MUMMIES
& THEIR MYSTERIES

MUMMIES
& THEIR MYSTERIES

CHARLOTTE WILCOX

BARNES
&NOBLE
BOOKS
NEW YORK

For my mother

Front cover: The peaceful expression on this bog mummy's face hides the story of his death.
Back cover (inset and detail): The mystery behind this small Egyptian mummy is revealed on page 22.
Page one: In later Egyptian mummies, the wrappings sometimes formed unusual patterns.
Page two: This Japanese priest tried to turn himself into a mummy before he died.
Page two and three (background): This woven mummy wrapping was found in a cave on the Aleutian Islands.

This edition published by Barnes & Noble, Inc.
by arrangement with Carolrhoda Books, Inc., a division of
the Lerner Publishing Group

1998 Barnes & Noble Books

Text copyright © 1993 by Charlotte Wilcox

Manufactured in the United States of America
1 2 3 4 5 6 – JR – 03 02 01 00 99 98

CONTENTS

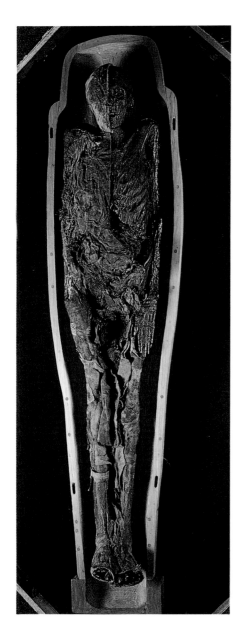

Egyptian mummies are famous all over the world. But Egypt is not the only place mummies have been found.

A little Arctic ground squirrel, shown above near its nest, was naturally mummified when it froze thousands of years ago.

CHAPTER ONE
WHAT IS A MUMMY?

If you are like most people, you probably picture a **mummy** wrapped in strips of ragged cloth, lying in the dusty corner of a museum or a dark passage in some Egyptian pyramid. The most famous ones are from Egypt, but mummies have been found all over the world. Some were buried with great care, but others became mummified because of natural conditions where they died.

A mummy is the body of a human or animal in which some of the soft tissues (skin, muscles, or organs) did not decay after death. This makes a mummy different from a skeleton or a fossil. A skeleton is only bones, with no soft tissues at all. A fossil keeps the shape of the human, animal, or plant, but the body itself has hardened into rock. Mummies are made naturally or by **embalming,** which is any process used to preserve a dead body.

While we are alive, our bodies fight off bacteria and fungi, but after death these germs and molds eat the body's tissues, causing decay. **Mummification** happens when bacteria and fungi cannot grow in the dead body. Most mummies, whether natural or embalmed, result when the body quickly dries out after death, because bacteria and fungi need water to live. Mummies can be dried in the sun, with chemicals, or with fire or smoke.

Drying isn't the only way to turn a body into a mummy. Taking away all air from around the body will stop decay, since bacteria and fungi need air as well as water to live. Quick, permanent freezing soon after

The skin and muscles of Egyptian mummies are hard and brittle because of **resin** used in embalming. Resin is a tree sap that works like glue—it is sticky when fresh, but becomes very hard when left out in the air. Even though they have become hard in many mummies, skin and muscles are called "soft tissues" because they were soft when the person was alive.

MUMMIES AROUND THE WORLD

Most areas of the world where mummies have been found (shaded brown) are either very dry or very cold.

death can produce mummies, because most bacteria cannot grow in below-freezing temperatures. Bodies can mummify if they are buried in soil containing chemicals that kill bacteria. Cool, dry air in some caves contains gases that kill bacteria and can make mummies naturally.

HOW WE GOT THE WORD *MUMMY*

When the word *mummy* was first used in the English language in the early 1400s, it did not mean a body as it does now. Instead, it was the name of a medicine. Mummy comes from *mumiyah,* an Arabic word for **bitumen**, a sticky oil now used to make roads.

In the Middle Ages, people in Europe thought bitumen could cure diseases. They also thought ancient Egyptians had used bitumen in mummy wrappings. This, people felt, gave bitumen extra healing power. Around 600 or 700 years ago, Europeans began grinding up mummy wrappings and selling the powder as a medicine. People put **mummy powder** on wounds to help them heal and even ate it in hopes of curing stomach troubles!

At first, only the wrappings were made into medicine. Later, whole bodies—thousands of them— were ground into powder. As old mummies became harder to find, Egyptians started making fake mummies from bodies of people who had recently died. They stuffed the bodies with

bitumen, wrapped them in linen, and dried them in the sun. When they were dry enough to look like real mummies, the bodies were sold to be ground into powder.

We now know that Egyptians used resin, not bitumen, in mummy wrappings. So the powder made from real mummies had no bitumen in it at all. Still, doctors all over Europe told patients to use mummy powder.

In the late 1500s, a doctor from France visited a factory that made fake mummies. When he learned that the Egyptians did not bother to find out how the people died, he was afraid. Fake mummies could carry diseases that could spread to people taking mummy powder as medicine. The Frenchman urged doctors to stop using mummy powder. Soon it was against the law to make fake mummies or to take mummies out of Egypt. This put the mummy makers out of business. People stopped using mummies for medicine, and by the 1600s the word came to mean what it does today—a preserved body.

WHY MUMMIES WERE MADE

Most people all over the world, in every period of history, have believed in life after death. Ideas change with time and place, but most people feel their spirits will outlast their bodies. They often see death as the beginning of another life.

For these reasons, people treat dead bodies with respect, care, and sometimes even with fear. Turning bodies into mummies is one of many different ways of caring for the dead.

People have made mummies for at least 5,000 years. Many believed the body they had in this life might be needed in the next. People have imagined dead bodies could do all sorts of things—from walking and talking to putting curses on living people. These superstitions are not true, but people all over the world still show respect for the dead.

Egyptian mummy wrappings —made mostly of linen and resin—have been used for medicine, in artists' paints, to make paper, and even for fuel!

HOW TO LOOK AT MUMMIES

You may have mixed feelings about seeing a mummy. When you look at the photographs in this book—or when you see mummies in a museum—they will probably seem very different from living people. It may be hard to imagine that a mummy was once a child who grew, learned, and loved a family just as you do. Anyone who wants to learn about mummies should keep two things in mind.

First, we must remember that a mummy was once a living person with thoughts and feelings much like ours. We respect what remains of that person's body, because it is similar to ours. Most religions ask that dead bodies be treated with dignity. Laughing or making jokes about the dead—even a mummy who died thousands of years ago—goes against the beliefs of many people throughout the world.

We must also remember that a mummy, though once really alive, is now *really dead.* A mummy can do absolutely nothing that a living body can do. It cannot see, hear, feel,

Coffins, boxes for burying dead bodies, have been used since ancient times. This Egyptian coffin is of wood—which was probably expensive because not many trees grow in Egypt. The symbols painted on it are **hieroglyphs,** a form of picture writing used in ancient Egypt.

or think. One thing a mummy can do is give us information about the past.

MUMMIES AND OUR PAST

Preserving the body cannot bring life after death, but researchers are uncovering secrets mummies have kept for thousands of years. The secrets mummies hold can tell us how people lived, how environment affected their health, and how modern people have built on the knowledge of their ancestors. Mummies let us look at our past in a way no other form of history—stories, letters, art, photographs, or other artifacts—can.

Soft tissues—found in mummies but not in skeletons—tell us about family traits, diet, and disease. Lungs can show what was in the air in ancient times. Stomach, liver, and intestine tissue can show what people ate. Bacteria and other causes of disease stay in soft tissues, giving clues about how diseases are caused and spread.

When put together like pieces in a puzzle, these clues can help solve mysteries from the past. Let's take a look at some of these mysteries.

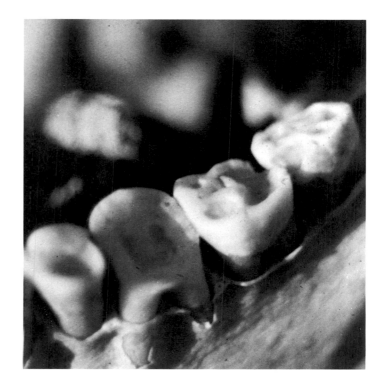

Teeth from ancient mummies are often worn down more than is common today. In desert areas like Egypt, where this mummy was found, blowing sand got into food and water, causing wear on the teeth. Not surprisingly, many people in ancient times had bad toothaches.

We've known for thousands of years why ancient Egyptians made mummies, but *how* they did it has long been a mystery.

CHAPTER TWO
THE MOST FAMOUS MUMMIES-EGYPT

Egyptian mummies have been the subject of legends for thousands of years. It was once believed that ancient Egyptians used secret spells to preserve bodies. No Egyptian writings have ever been found telling exactly how Egyptians made mummies. But a Greek writer, Herodotus, visited Egypt over 2,000 years ago and saw mummies being embalmed. Thanks to Herodotus and to modern research, the process the Egyptians used is no longer a mystery.

The oldest Egyptian mummies, from before 2500 B.C., were not embalmed at all. They became mummies naturally.

In early times, bodies were simply wrapped in cloth or leather and buried in the sand. Warm desert winds and hot sun heating the sand caused bodies to dry out very quickly, so they did not decay.

Even very early in their history, Egyptians believed in life after death. Pottery and jewelry were put in graves for the dead to use. Over time, this belief grew into a religion. As the Egyptian religion grew, so did the importance of taking care of the dead.

Egyptian kings, called **pharaohs,** were thought to be gods. When a pharaoh died, Egyptians thought his spirit turned into Osiris, god-king of the dead. The dead pharaoh's son became ruler of Egypt in his place. Egyptians called their ruler Horus, god-king of the living.

In order for the pharaoh's spirit to live in the spirit world, Egyptians thought it had to have a body to rest in on earth. They thought that if the body looked something like the pharaoh did when he was alive, his spirit would recognize it.

During his life, a pharaoh made lavish preparations for the life he expected to live after death. He stored food, clothing, books, medicine, gold and jewels, weapons, furniture, and other things he enjoyed in life.

Osiris, in mummy wrappings and wearing a crown, sits on his throne. A woman offers him an eye on a platter. Their green skin color shows that the two are living in the world of the dead.

 # THE LEGEND OF OSIRIS AND ISIS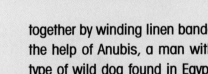

Ancient Egyptians believed that Osiris, a good and wise king, was the first pharaoh. He spread knowledge to other parts of the world, while his wife, Isis, ruled Egypt in his place. Upon returning home, Osiris was murdered by his evil brother, Set, who cut his body into pieces and dumped it in the Nile River. Isis found the body and put it back together by winding linen bandages around it. Then, with the help of Anubis, a man with the head of a jackal (a type of wild dog found in Egypt), Isis breathed life back into Osiris. He could not return to the land of the living, but entered the spirit world and became god of the dead. Anubis became the god of embalming.

Egyptians believed that the spirits of the dead needed their own houses. At first this was done by building underground rooms, called tombs, where the body and other things were buried. Later pharaohs built rooms or houses over the tombs. As each pharaoh tried to outdo the ones before, the houses became larger and more beautiful.

The largest of all the tomb houses were the pyramids. Over 70 pharaohs built pyramids for themselves. The Great Pyramid, built by Pharaoh Khufu over 4,000 years ago, is still the largest stone structure in the world. Until about a hundred years ago, it was also the world's tallest building.

HOW TO MAKE AN EGYPTIAN MUMMY

By about 2500 B.C., Egyptian priests were embalming bodies by drying them with salt. (This was not a mystery to Egyptians, because they preserved meat by drying it in the sun or by packing it in salt.) Working under large tents, embalmers took 70 days to prepare a body for burial.

1. The first step was to remove the organs. These parts of the body decay first. Embalmers used a long metal rod to take brain tissue out through the nose. They did not save the brain in most cases and usually left the heart inside the body. (Ancient Egyptians believed people's thoughts came from the heart muscle and not the brain.) Embalmers also took out the lungs, stomach, liver, and intestines through a cut in the side.

2. The body was washed inside and out with wine, which contains alcohol and kills bacteria. (Even though Egyptians probably didn't know about bacteria, they cleaned cuts with wine.) The body was then stuffed with cloth or other material to help it dry and keep its shape.

3. The lungs, stomach, liver, and intestines were washed, dried, and covered with resin. They were then wrapped in linen and put in separate jars—called **canopic jars**—made of stone, pottery, or wood. Some jars had human or animal faces carved on the lids. The jars were later buried near the mummy.

4. Next came the most important step of all—complete drying of the body. Embalmers packed the body in **natron,** a type of salt similar to what is now used in water softeners. Just as salty foods make us thirsty, natron sucks water out of the tissues. Embalmers covered the body with natron for 40 days. Since so much of the human body is water, removing it makes the body

thin and the skin like leather. Removing water from the body was the key step in making an Egyptian mummy.

5. After drying, the stuffing was taken out and replaced with new linen stuffing plus small bags filled with natron, sawdust, earth, or herbs. The cut in the side was closed and linen pads or jewels were put over the eyes. Oil, perfume, and spices were rubbed on the skin.

6. The entire body was then smeared with warm resin. As it cooled, the resin became very hard. This sealed the skin in a hard coating and kept water from getting in.

7. Next the body was decorated with bracelets, rings, and necklaces. Fingernails and toenails were painted or covered with gold or silver. Hair was styled and makeup put on.

8. Then the task of wrapping began. About 150 yards of long linen strips were used. The strips sometimes had hieroglyphs and other symbols on them. First, narrow strips

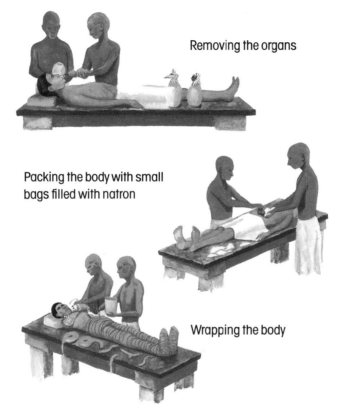

Removing the organs

Packing the body with small bags filled with natron

Wrapping the body

were wound around each finger and toe separately, then around each hand and arm, foot and leg. Resin was added between the layers of cloth to make them stick together. More jewels and charms were sometimes put in the wrappings. An outer layer of linen strips was wound around the entire body and head, then fastened with straps, buttons, or jewels. The layers of cloth and resin formed a hard casing, like papier-mâché, called the cartonnage. A human face was often painted on the cartonnage, or a mask was placed over the head.

9. Finally, the mummy was put in a series of coffins, each one nested inside the other. A typical coffin was brightly painted with words, pictures, and a human head. Coffins were made of wood or stone, sometimes covered with gold. Stone was often used for the outside container, with wooden coffins nested inside. Flowers, books, or food were placed inside many coffins.

THE EGYPTIAN FUNERAL

Once the mummy was ready, the public part of the funeral took place. Special servants, called mourners, were hired to cry very loudly as the body was taken from the embalming tent to the tomb. Some pharaohs built special temples near their tombs. Religious ceremonies and sacrifices to Egyptian gods were held. Priests performed a ceremony they thought would help the mummy see, hear, eat, and drink again in the spirit world.

After the funeral, the tomb was closed and sealed. It was not to be disturbed. Unfortunately, some Egyptians didn't follow this rule. Workers built secret passages into some pyramids so they could rob them later. Some coffins had secret trap doors built into them for the same reason. Almost all the tombs of the pharaohs were robbed in ancient times. Grave robbers looking for treasure unwrapped many Egyptian mummies. When family members or caretakers found the damage, they had embalmers repair and rewrap the bodies.

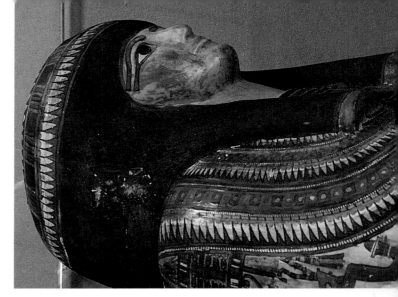

Lady Tashat, as this mummy is called, belonged to an important Egyptian family.

As the practice of mummy embalming continued, bodies of royal wives, officials, and priests were also made into mummies, with the hope that they would join the pharaohs in the spirit world. Soon other wealthy Egyptians arranged to have their bodies mummified when they died.

Over time, almost all Egyptians who could afford it became mummies—more than 70 million mummies in about 3,000 years. The Egyptians stopped making mummies around the fourth century A.D. By that time, many Egyptians had become Christians, so they no longer believed mummification was necessary for life after death.

THE MYSTERY OF LADY TASHAT

Lady Tashat was a well-to-do Egyptian girl who lived about 3,000 years ago. She was a teenager when she died. Tashat became a mummy because she came from an important Egyptian family.

When the mummy of Lady Tashat was x-rayed in 1916, shocked researchers saw an extra head inside the coffin, resting between her legs. They could only guess why it was there.

The mystery was not solved until new research tools were invented. **CT scans** taken in 1983 show that Tashat's body had been rewrapped sometime after it was embalmed, probably to repair damage done by grave robbers. The extra head may be all that is left of another body. The CT scan below shows a cross section of Tashat and the extra head. The extra skull is the large circle in the middle. The two circles near the bottom are Tashat's leg bones, with the bones of her ten fingers above them. Wrappings fill the rest of the picture, and the coffin makes up the outer circle.

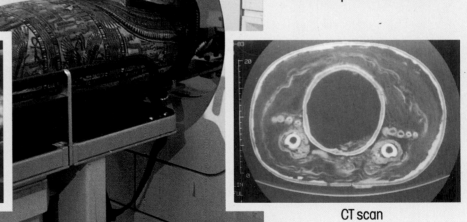

X ray

CT scan

What's this mummy's mystery? A human face was painted on the small mummy above, but the body inside is a hawk about 18 inches long. The hawk was a symbol of the sun-god, Re.

ANIMAL MUMMIES

Ancient Egyptians believed many animals were sacred. Embalmers sold mummified animals to use as offerings in religious ceremonies. Mummified cats were buried near many shrines of the cat-goddess, Bastet. Sacred crocodiles—kept in pools near temples of the crocodile-god, Sobek—were embalmed when they died. Bulls, beetles, dogs, bats, shrews, and even fish became mummies. Over a million bird mummies were buried in one cemetery alone.

The popularity of animal mummies may explain one mystery from Egypt's past—the disappearance of one kind of ancient ibis. This long-beaked water bird was special to the Egyptians because it returned to Egypt each year at the beginning of the growing season. Now the bird is extinct, probably because so many were killed by the ancient Egyptians to make mummies.

Left: The ibis, a water bird, was special to the Egyptians. This ibis mummy has been unwrapped.

CHAPTER THREE

MILLIONS OF MUMMIES—
THE INCAN EMPIRE

About the time Egyptians began making mummies, ancestors of the Incas were developing their own way of caring for the dead. They practiced embalming as early as Egyptians, but continued more than a thousand years longer.

The Incas lived in western South America at the time of Columbus. The desert coastland where they lived is perhaps the driest place on earth. This region may hold more mummies than anywhere in the world except Egypt.

Like many ancient people, Incas buried food, clothing, and other items with the dead. This little boy was buried with (from left) a bag of coca leaves; a silver statue with a cap made of parrot feathers; two small llamas; and five little pouches holding his baby teeth, hair, and fingernail clippings.

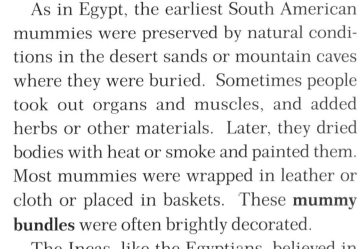

As in Egypt, the earliest South American mummies were preserved by natural conditions in the desert sands or mountain caves where they were buried. Sometimes people took out organs and muscles, and added herbs or other materials. Later, they dried bodies with heat or smoke and painted them. Most mummies were wrapped in leather or cloth or placed in baskets. These **mummy bundles** were often brightly decorated.

The Incas, like the Egyptians, believed in life after death and worshiped their king as a god. By around the year 1400, Incan rulers were embalmed when they died and seated on thrones in beautiful tombs. Servants brought the mummies food, washed and

The Incas and their ancestors used mummy bundles like this one. The body sits with the knees drawn up to the chest, making a bulge in the middle. The smaller bulge at the bottom is the feet.

changed their clothing, and let visitors in to see them. Royal mummies were paraded through the streets on special days.

When Europeans came to the Incan Empire, they found gold, silver, and copper mines, and many other treasures. Spanish soldiers conquered the land in the 1500s and 1600s, forcing the Incas to work as slaves in fields and mines they once owned. Soldiers destroyed royal mummies, because they were symbols of Incan rule.

Still, thousands of mummies of common people remain. Some found near Pisco, in modern-day Peru, tell the story of the Incas' lives after Spanish explorers and fortune hunters came to their land.

This drawing from the early 1600s shows the mummy of an Incan ruler being carried in a parade. The Spanish words tell of the Incan Festival of the Dead during the month of November.

INCAN MUMMIES TELL THEIR STORY

Recently a team of researchers studied about 70 Incan mummies buried near Pisco. Old Spanish records tell how the Spanish government worked to bring Christianity—and Christian beliefs about caring for the dead—to the Incas. The Pisco mummies were from the time of Spanish rule, but they were still buried in traditional Incan mummy bundles.

The researchers uncovered other, very disturbing things in the Pisco graves. They found 15 times as many females as males buried near the village. All the able-bodied men had left— possibly to work in Spanish mines. The few men and boys who stayed had physical handicaps.

Because so few men were buried in the village, researchers think most never returned home after being taken to the mines. Those who did had dangerous traces of silver, copper, and iron in their lungs.

This man died in a copper mine in northern Chile. Copper salts in the mine preserved his body and turned it green.

Several men had died of lung diseases. This could have been caused by breathing unhealthy air for long days in the mines.

All the Pisco mummies showed signs that they did not have enough food. Their clothes were ragged and patched. Saddest of all, almost every mummy found near Pisco had broken bones—500 times more broken bones than people had before the Spanish soldiers came. Modern research on the Pisco mummies tells the story of the Spanish soldiers' cruelty better than reports written at the time.

MUMMIES AND THE LIVING

Mummies from the Incan region have not only answered questions about the past. They have also solved problems of the present.

A research team found that many mummies near Arica, Chile, had suffered, and perhaps died, from arsenic poisoning. Arsenic is a metal found in rocks and soil. The mummies had been poisoned not just at one time, but over hundreds of years—a clue that the arsenic probably came from the environment. Was the poison still there?

Researchers told local officials about the poisoned mummies. They gave blood tests to people living in the village and found arsenic in their blood. Next the water was tested. A stream brought water into the village, carrying with it arsenic from the mountain soil above. When they learned of the danger, the villagers stopped using water from the stream and found a new water supply. Through the arsenic still present in their soft tissues, mummies gave their living neighbors warnings and clues to a deadly mystery.

CHAPTER FOUR

AMERICA'S BURIED TREASURES –THE CAVE MUMMIES

Caves and rock shelters hold many treasures, including some preserved bodies of native North Americans. Mummies have been found in several places—from Alaska to Greenland to the American Southwest.

Most of these mummies were carefully laid to rest by relatives or friends. These people probably didn't know that the bodies they took to the caves would be preserved for hundreds or thousands of years. Mummification was not usually planned, but happened because of natural conditions. In a few cases, people were accidentally trapped or injured in the caves, which then became their tombs.

Native Americans mined minerals in caves for hundreds of years. Many carried climbing sticks, like the one shown at left with a researcher in Mammoth Cave. A number of bodies have also been found in caves, but why they were placed there is not clear.

The mummified body of a nine-year-old Native American boy was found on this ledge deep inside the Flint Mammoth Cave system, in an area known as Mummy Valley. It takes over two hours by foot to reach the spot where he was placed, with the only light coming from lanterns and torches.

THE FLINT MAMMOTH CAVE MUMMIES

The Flint Mammoth Cave system is the longest in the world, with 145 miles of caverns and tunnels carved by water out of limestone rocks beneath central Kentucky. Dry air moves through the caves, and the temperature—about 50° Fahrenheit—never changes. Valuable minerals have been mined there since ancient times. Dryness, cool temperatures, and minerals that contain salt help keep bodies in the caves from decaying.

Several mummies have been found in the Flint Mammoth Cave chain since the early 1800s. These and other mummies from Kentucky and Tennessee have been removed from the caves where they rested. Some were studied by researchers. All are now protected from the effects of time and from the curious eyes of tourists and explorers.

Most ancient North American people greatly respected the dead. They treated the dead with dignity. Burial was an important ceremony. Most often the early Native Americans wrapped the dead in blankets or dressed them in special clothes. They laid the bodies in graves, outdoor shelters, or beneath mounds of earth.

Researchers don't know why early Americans carried only a few people deep inside caves and carefully placed them on rock ledges—or if they knew the bodies would be preserved there. Perhaps future research will shed light on this mystery.

In the 1800s, new settlers in Kentucky began exploring the Mammoth Cave system. Over the years, they discovered several mummified bodies. When looters removed one such mummy, J. M. Smith carved this outraged message on the cave wall: "You low down scoundrls. What is it you wouldn't do?... Sir, you are worse than a murderer. Are you not afraid it will follow you in your paths of a day and your bed at night?"

Two rancher brothers from Colorado explored Anasazi cliff houses in the late 1800s. One of the brothers is shown standing near the entrance to a cliff house where mummies were found in what is now Mesa Verde National Park.

THE BASKET MAKER MUMMIES

The Four Corners region — where Arizona, New Mexico, Colorado, and Utah meet — has more mummies than anywhere else in the United States. Ranchers found the first mummy in 1889 in what is now Mesa Verde National Park, Colorado. This mummy was from a group of early Native Americans called Anasazi, which means ancient people in the Navaho language. The Anasazi were ancestors of the Pueblo Indians who now live in the region.

Scientists often call early Anasazi people Basket Makers, because they used baskets so much in their everyday lives. The Anasazi Basket Makers used dry mountain caves as homes, storage rooms, and burial chambers. The very dry conditions in these caves caused some bodies to become mummies.

The oldest Basket Maker mummies found in Arizona caves are 1,500 to 2,000 years old, and the latest about 600 years old. These mummies span a long time, but they have some things in common. They were all found wrapped in fur or leather blankets, either in caves or rock holes.

The Anasazi, like many other ancient peoples, believed in life after death. They often buried a new pair of sandals with the dead, showing hope that the person would rise and walk again in the next life.

THE WARM CAVES OF ALASKA

While the Anasazi built cave cities in the Southwest, another group of Native Americans developed their own burial customs in caves far to the north. The Aleut people lived on the Aleutian Islands off the coast of present-day Alaska. They were related to the Inuit people of the Alaskan mainland but had their own language and customs — including making mummies. Just as in other places, Aleut embalming grew out of a belief in life after death.

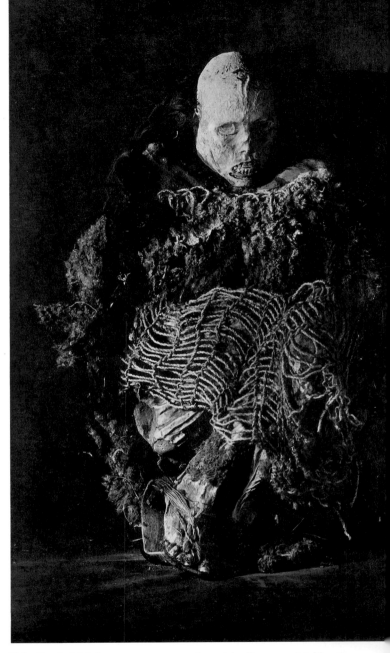

This Basket Maker mummy was found in Canyon del Muerto, "the Canyon of the Dead," in what is now Arizona.

The Aleutian Islands are the tops of old volcanoes in the Pacific Ocean. Warm winds and water from the south meet cold air and icy water from the Arctic north. The weather is the same most of the time—foggy, rainy, and very windy. The temperature stays just above freezing all year long, but heat from volcanoes beneath the surface keeps some island caves very warm and dry. Conditions in the Aleutian climate are just right for making mummies naturally.

When Aleuts wanted to mummify a dead person, they usually removed organs and stuffed the inside of the body with dry grass. The next step was to lay the body in a stream. The running water dissolved the fat and washed it away, leaving only muscle and skin. Then the body was tied in a squatting position and dried in the air.

The dry mummy was wrapped in several layers of waterproof leather and woven clothing, then tied around the outside with

In 1990, researchers from Vassar College excavated a burial cave on the Aleutian Islands. Along with bodies hundreds of years old, they found grass matting (left) used as mummy wrappings and several wooden sculptures. The sculpture below shows a killer whale with an Aleut hunter in its mouth.

a braided cord. It was placed in a warm cave, either hanging from the ceiling or lying on a platform to keep it off the damp floor. Many bodies were preserved for several hundred years in this way.

Scientists estimate the Aleuts used caves for burial for only a few hundred years. They may have embalmed bodies for a much longer time. How long they used embalming is a mystery, because the only bodies that survived were in the caves. One Aleutian cave held more than 50 mummies that are about 250 years old. The Aleutian folktale below explains why they were buried there.

THE TALE OF LITTLE WREN

A chief named Little Wren lived near a warm Aleutian cave. One day, his young son was accidentally killed by his brother-in-law. As the family was going to the funeral, Little Wren's daughter slipped on a rock, causing her baby to die. Little Wren buried his son and the baby together in the nearby cave. Little Wren was so heartbroken that he soon died. He too was buried in the cave, which over time became the burial place for all his family.

Scientists guessed this tiny Greenland mummy is a boy, but were too moved by his delicate beauty to examine the body. He was extremely well preserved, probably because a small body cools off sooner after death. Larger bodies hold heat longer, allowing more bacteria to grow and destroy the tissues.

THE MUMMIES OF GREENLAND

On the opposite side of North America, another island cave also held mummies—but the cause of preservation was entirely different from the Aleutian mummies. On the western coast of icy Greenland, mountains rise up near an abandoned Inuit village. Two hunters wandered into the area in 1972 and discovered a cave with eight mummified bodies. The six women and two children are among the best-preserved human bodies ever found in North America. They lived about 500 years ago.

The Greenland mummies were not embalmed, as the mummies on the Aleutian Islands were. Instead, they were well dressed and carefully laid on sealskin blankets in the cave, protected from rain, snow, and sun. Drying ocean winds and cold temperatures kept the bodies from decaying.

The bodies of the Greenland mummies hold many clues about their lives—what they ate, the type of air they breathed, and what diseases they had. The greatest mystery about the Greenland mummies is how they died. One woman had cancer, but none had other diseases that would have killed them. They did not drown and were not killed in accidents. Maybe they froze to death or died of food poisoning, but for now these are only guesses.

The body of this Greenland woman gives clues to her great courage. Her front teeth were worn down from a lifetime of holding things in her mouth while working. A broken collarbone had never healed. She had cancer that left her blind in one eye and deaf. Scientists believe she was in great pain. Even so, her mummified hands show she kept working right up to her death: her thumbnail still has marks from cutting thread across it.

CHAPTER FIVE

FROZEN IN TIME—
MUMMIES PRESERVED IN ICE

Frozen mummies have been found near both the North and South Poles and in the mountains of Europe and Asia. When bodies freeze soon after death, they can stay very well preserved until they thaw out—even if that doesn't happen for thousands of years. A few of these frozen bodies have already solved puzzles from the past. Others still keep their mysteries.

THE MYSTERIOUS DEATHS OF SAILORS AND EXPLORERS

English Navy Captain Robert Falcon Scott and two of his men died while returning from an expedition to the South Pole in 1912. No one knew what had happened to them until a search party reached their camp months later. The leader of the rescue team was a

Rescuers found the bodies of English explorer Robert Scott and his men lying in their tent near the South Pole. The rescuers folded the tent over the dead men, covered it with snow, and topped it with a cross. Why the explorers died remains a frozen mystery to this day.

doctor, but he didn't examine the bodies.

The team's food and fuel were almost gone when they died, even though they were only 11 miles from extra supplies. Why did they stay in the tent for over a week when supplies were so close? Why didn't at least one of them try to reach the supplies?

Captain Scott and the other explorers kept records and diaries. Much of their equipment has been saved. But the most important clues may still be buried in their frozen bodies.

The deaths of the Antarctic explorers are a mystery, but the bodies of another team of English explorers—from the opposite end of the globe—give some clues. An English sailing crew was mapping the Northwest

Passage in northern Canada about 150 years ago. In the fall of 1846, their two large ships were caught in ice 15 miles offshore. A year and a half later, they were still trapped. By the spring of 1848, the captain and 24 of the sailors had died.

The ships had plenty of food, so why did so many sailors die? And why did 105 of them start off on foot toward a trading post 1,000 miles south, when they knew whaling ships would be passing by closer to the north? Why did they drag along lifeboats filled with useless things—curtain rods, dinnerware, a desk, and other heavy items— but leave behind needed clothing and gloves?

These questions were unanswered until researchers dug up the frozen bodies of three

Seaman John Hartnell (left) died three days after New Year's Day, 1846. His body and that of John Torrington (opposite, right) were almost perfectly preserved in the permanently frozen ground on Beechey Island.

men on Beechey Island, 500 miles inside the Arctic Circle. In 1984, the grave of one of the sailors, John Torrington, was opened. The grave had been dug several feet down into permanently frozen gravel. The body was in a well-made wooden coffin and was completely frozen.

Tissue samples gave researchers one of the clues they were looking for. Torrington's body contained five times more lead than normal for the place and time in which he died. Still, scientists did not know where the lead came from—or what, if anything, it had to do with the sailor's death. More clues were needed.

Researchers returned to Beechey Island in 1986. They examined the frozen bodies of two more explorers, John Hartnell and William Braine. Both men were so thin they seemed to be starving. Each weighed less than 100 pounds. Both had empty stomachs and intestines, showing they had not eaten for some time before they died. After taking tissue samples, researchers carefully buried the bodies again exactly as they found them.

The samples were taken to a laboratory and found to have high levels of lead.

Researchers uncovered another important clue in the explorers' garbage dump. They found tin food cans sealed with lead, which could have seeped into the food. During their terrible journey, the crew ate thousands of cans of food sealed with lead.

Tin cans unearthed on Beechey Island were the single most important clue in discovering why sailors mapping the Northwest Passage in the 1840s died.

Lead poisoning has been a problem for thousands of years and still is today. Lead is a metal found in earth and rocks. Tiny amounts enter the body through the air or in food. As long as the amounts are small, lead does not cause harm. But if the body takes in too much lead over a long time, it builds up and is dangerous. Victims first feel weak and lose their appetites. Some victims have brain damage that causes mental problems. They may be unable to move or may shake horribly. People can die from severe lead poisoning.

Scientists believe the Northwest Passage sailors were unable to make wise decisions because of lead in their diets. This would explain why they went the wrong way and brought the wrong supplies with them.

Some researchers think that Captain Scott and his men were also victims of their diets. A lack of vitamins and calories may have taken away their energy and made them unable to stand the cold of Antarctica. It could even have caused them to make the poor decisions that led to their deaths.

When modern-day hikers in Italy saw the head and shoulders of a man sticking out of the snow, they had no idea they had just discovered the oldest mummified body in Europe.

HIKER IN THE ALPS

The frozen bodies of men who died near the North and South Poles date back only about 150 years. Other frozen mummies tell about conditions much earlier. Among the oldest is the body of a mountain climber who died high in the Alps of Italy about 5,000 years ago. He was frozen in a glacier until 1991. Modern-day mountain climbers noticed his head and shoulders sticking out of the ice.

The body was found resting on a rock in a nine-foot-deep trench. This kept it from being damaged by the moving glacier. There was no ice in the trench when the man died there. The ice must have filled in very soon after and not melted until 1991. A few hundred years ago, glaciers in the Alps were as small as they are now. Somehow, the body must have been protected from melting at that time.

The hikers who found the body had no idea it was so old—they thought the man might have been recently murdered. Police were called, but before they got there tourists had taken parts of the mummy and his clothing for souvenirs. By the time scientists arrived, most of the man's clothes had been ripped up and his body had been badly damaged.

Five days after it was found, the mummy was finally moved to cold storage at a university in Austria. There scientists began to piece the clothing and body back together. They found three tattoos, plus hair samples showing that the man had cut his hair. These are the oldest known examples of tattoos and haircuts in the world.

The man was healthy and had no wounds. Scientists guess he froze to death when he was caught in a snowstorm. Researchers all over the world are studying tiny samples of the mummy's body tissue for more clues about what the oldest known European ate, how he lived, and how he died.

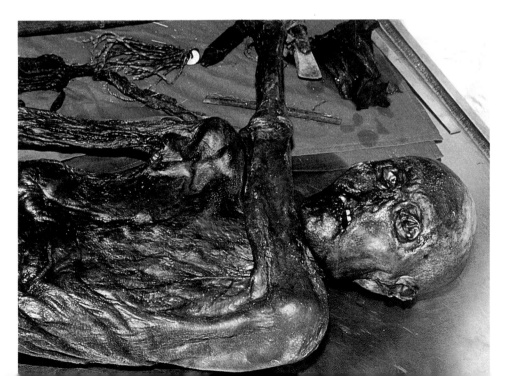

The oldest known European wore a finely stitched leather and fur suit, leather boots, and a stone necklace. Over this he wore a cape woven from grass. He carried an ax, knife, leather pouch, bow and arrows, several pieces of flint, berries, and two mushrooms. The mushrooms are a kind known to fight disease. Scientists believe the man carried the mushrooms to be used as medicine.

This Scythian ruler lived about 2,500 years ago in what is now southern Russia.

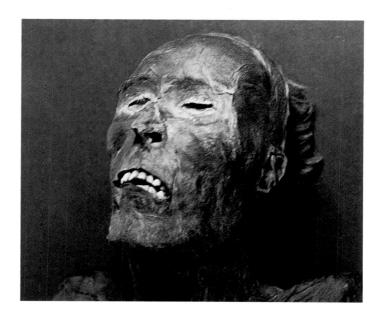

MOUNTAIN NOMADS

High in the mountains of southern Russia, human and animal bodies have been found in chilly graves. These are the bodies of Scythian rulers and their horses. The Scythians were nomads who roamed on horseback throughout southern Russia over 2,000 years ago.

Herodotus, the Greek writer, visited the Scythians and wrote about the way they embalmed their kings. Scythians generally removed the organs, stuffed the inside of the body with herbs, and sealed it with wax. Preparations were elaborate but didn't work very well. Some of these bodies were preserved—but not because of the embalming Herodotus wrote about.

Large graves—sometimes two stories deep —were dug in the earth and lined with wood and rock. The ruler, some of his favorite horses, and treasures were placed in the grave. Workers built a wooden roof over it and covered the entire grave with dirt and stones, hoping to protect the body from damage. Some mummies did survive for thousands of years—but only because of cracks in the graves. Water ran into many graves and filled them with ice, freezing and preserving the Scythian mummies.

A FAMILY IN ALASKA

A terrible Arctic storm hit the coast of northern Alaska about 450 years ago. Tons of packed ice crashed against the shore near what is now Barrow, Alaska. In 1982, treasure hunters from Barrow chopped into the ice and found more than antiques. Two women, a teenage boy, and two girls lay frozen in their beds. The five—all members of one Inuit family—died instantly when huge ice chunks buried their house.

A parka made of caribou skin was found in an Inuit family home destroyed by an ice storm about 450 years ago.

The Inuit family left behind many clues about the life they lived. Winter supplies had been neatly put away. The family had plenty of food and clothing and were all fairly healthy. Researchers found a comb, buttons, and what might have been a child's doll.

Scientists discovered that someone, perhaps a relative, came in after the storm and took out some food and tools. Then that person left the house and the family as they were. One woman had been nursing a baby before she died, but it was not in the ruins. Maybe the baby's body was too small to have been preserved in the crashing ice. Or maybe the baby was rescued and adopted by another family.

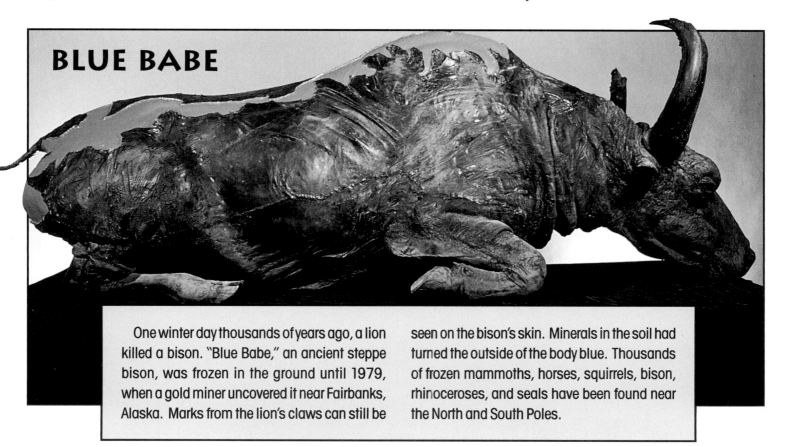

BLUE BABE

One winter day thousands of years ago, a lion killed a bison. "Blue Babe," an ancient steppe bison, was frozen in the ground until 1979, when a gold miner uncovered it near Fairbanks, Alaska. Marks from the lion's claws can still be seen on the bison's skin. Minerals in the soil had turned the outside of the body blue. Thousands of frozen mammoths, horses, squirrels, bison, rhinoceroses, and seals have been found near the North and South Poles.

CHAPTER SIX

TO HONOR THE PAST— MUMMIES OF THE FAR EAST

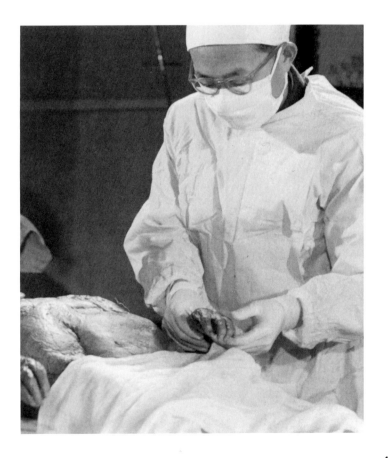

When you think of ancient Japan and China, you might think of samurai warriors, but probably not mummies. Ancient Orientals went to great lengths to honor the dead, but preserving the body was not as important as preserving the memory of the person. Still, a few mummies—including one of the best-preserved mummies in the world—have survived.

China's only mummy was so well preserved that her arms bent easily. Her body held many clues about how she lived and why she died. But who she was remains a mystery.

Seven nested coffins rested on a bed of 26 bamboo mats in this ancient Chinese tomb. A layer of waterproof white clay sealed the grave. Below that, tons of charcoal soaked up any water before it could reach the coffins. The grave was covered with a huge pile of earth, on which trees grew in modern times.

THE ONLY CHINESE MUMMY

Many early Chinese rulers built beautiful tombs, covered with gold and silver, for themselves and their families. Two such tombs stood for 2,100 years in the city of Ch'ang-sha, China. Mounds of earth as tall as four-story buildings covered each tomb. When scientists dug into one mound in 1982, they found a fantastic treasure of art, clothing, household goods, and musical instruments.

Beneath a hill of dirt, five tons of charcoal, three feet of clay, seven nested coffins, and twenty layers of silk cloth, researchers found the greatest treasure of all. It was the body of an ancient Chinese woman, covered with liquid and sealed in an airtight grave.

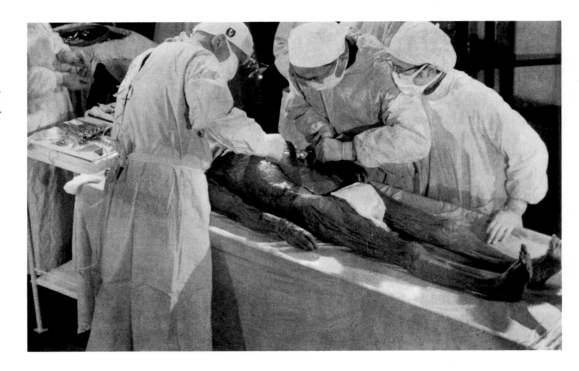

Doctors examined the oldest Asian mummy to discover the exact cause of her death.

The Chinese woman is unusual because her body never dried out. Scientists aren't sure whether she was preserved because of mercury (which kills bacteria) in the coffin, or because no air reached the body (bacteria need air to grow). This is probably the best-preserved body from ancient times found anywhere in the world. Doctors who examined the body were even able to bend her elbows and knees!

The woman was about 50 years old when she died. Like many people from ancient times, she suffered from tooth wear caused by a diet of seeds and nuts. She also had a lung disease and parasites, both common in ancient times. A lump on her spine probably caused her backaches. Paintings in the tomb show her walking with a cane.

Her well-preserved body gave scientists all the clues they needed to see that she died of a heart attack. Herbal medicine found in the tomb is similar to what Chinese herbal doctors still use for heart disease. Some scientists believe heart disease is caused mostly by modern eating and living habits. The Chinese mummy proves it affected people thousands of years ago.

Although researchers knew how the woman died, finding out who she was in life was not as easy. At first they thought the woman was the wife of a local official named Litsang. If that is true, then the tomb next to it probably contains her husband. Now some scientists believe the body is Lady Ch'eng, a wife of Emperor Ching, who ruled China over 2,000 years ago. Chinese history states that this princess was buried at Ch'ang-sha alongside one of her maids who was a special friend. If the mummy is Lady Ch'eng, then the other tomb probably holds her maid. Until the second tomb is opened, no one will know for sure.

MUMMIES IN JAPAN

Even though only one Chinese mummy has been found, Chinese Buddhists practiced mummy embalming for centuries. Their beliefs spread to Japan, where 19 mummies have survived. Some are almost 1,000 years old, the latest less than 100.

Most Japanese mummies were Buddhist priests who started their own mummification while they were still alive. A priest who hoped to become a mummy would gradually eat and drink less and less over a period

Melon seeds found in the stomach of China's only mummy show what the woman ate before she died.

As a young man, Tetsumonkai killed a samurai in a fight over a woman. He ran for safety to a temple and lived the rest of his life as a Buddhist priest. He died in 1829 after three years on a starvation diet.

of three years. By the end of three years, he would be eating and drinking almost nothing and would die.

Other priests then dried the body with smoke and buried it in a barrel. After three years it was taken out. Sometimes the skin was painted with ink or dye. Most bodies were seated as if in prayer, dressed in religious robes, and placed in temples. Some are still worshiped. Priest Koshi of Teradomari City, Japan, died 600 years ago, but worshipers still take his mummy out every October 2 for a religious ceremony.

The starvation diet followed by priests in Japan was supposed to keep the body from decaying after death, but modern scientists can't prove it worked. Buddhists no longer practice mummification, so whether or not a special diet can help make a mummy remains a mystery.

CHAPTER SEVEN
THE BOG PEOPLE—EUROPE'S MYSTERY

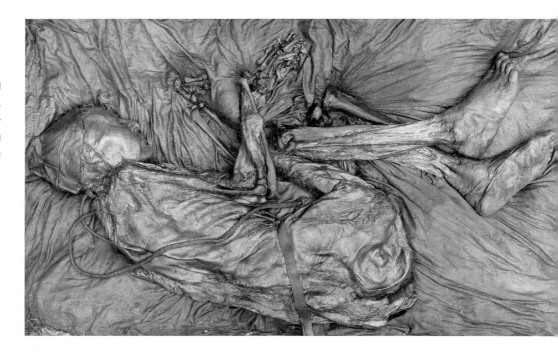

When farmers found this body in a Danish bog in 1950, they immediately called police. The 2,000-year-old body was so well preserved, the farmers thought the man had been recently murdered. The rope used to hang him was still around his neck.

Bogs are found all over the world, but only in Europe are bogs known to hold mummies. Nearly 2,000 preserved bodies have been pulled from bogs in Ireland, England, Norway, Denmark, Germany, Russia, and the island of Crete.

HOW BOGS MAKE MUMMIES

Below: *Peat has just been cut and removed from a bog in Ireland.*

Bogs form in low areas of land where water runs in and cannot drain out. Dead plants pile up at the bottom. Over time, the layers of soggy plants pack down and turn into **peat**, which looks like dark soil.

Mosses grow over the top of the bog, holding water between their tiny, sponge-like leaves. The trapped water in the mosses breaks down and loses its oxygen. Mosses give off acids that kill bacteria. The combination of acid and lack of oxygen keeps bacteria from growing and preserves bodies.

Acids in peat turn skin a dark brown and make hair and wool clothing a rusty red.

Most bog bodies were uncovered several feet down in a peat bed, an area of bog where chunks of peat are cut from the earth. Since ancient times, people have cut chunks of peat and used the dried blocks for fuel. From time to time, people cutting chunks of peat have found bodies instead of fuel. Not many bog bodies have been found since the 1950s, however, because fewer and fewer people burn peat in their stoves.

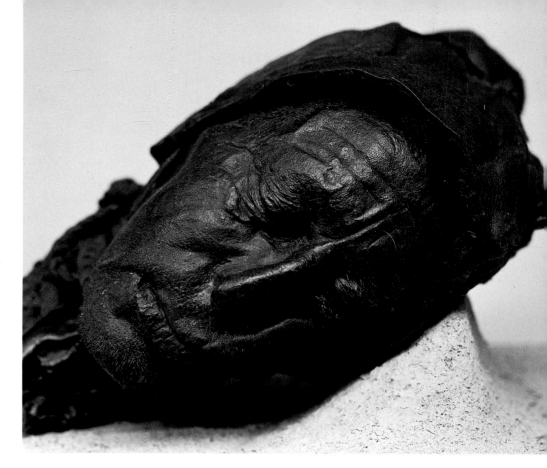

Even though he was strangled, this man was carefully placed in a sleeping position, his mouth and eyes thoughtfully closed by whoever put him there. The peaceful expression on his face is different from the pained look of most bog mummies.

DENMARK'S BOG BODIES

More bog mummies have been found in Denmark and northern Germany than anywhere else in the world. Most of Denmark's bog bodies are between 1,500 and 2,500 years old. And most show signs of violent death.

Several bog mummies were hanged or strangled with a rope. Some had their skulls crushed. One woman was scalped. One man was beheaded, another was stabbed, and another's throat was slit. All were thrown into the bogs, and some had sticks or branches piled on top of them as if to keep them from getting up.

Still, some scientists think the bog mummies may have been people who were favored in the community. They were well dressed.

Their hands look as if they did not work hard during their lives. So why were they killed?

Ancient Europeans believed gods lived in the bogs. People made human sacrifices to their gods. The mummies could have been sacrificed to bog gods, perhaps in early spring hoping for a good growing season, or during a winter celebration after a peat harvest. Evidence from the mummies' stomachs supports this idea. Several mummies had eaten a soup made of grain and seeds just before they died. Because they ate no fresh vegetables, fruits, or berries, scientists believe they died in winter or early spring.

Or were the bog mummies executed for crimes? Writers from their time report that people threw criminals into bogs. Were the mummies victims of violent crimes themselves? For now, the answers to these questions may still be buried in the bogs.

Danish police took fingerprints from this bog mummy. His fingerprint pattern is still common in Denmark, even though he lived 2,000 years ago.

Women's clothing in ancient Europe was not that different from modern European clothing. This lambskin cape and checkered wool skirt came from a bog.

Beneath this woman's beautifully braided hair, marks from the rope that hanged her can still be seen.

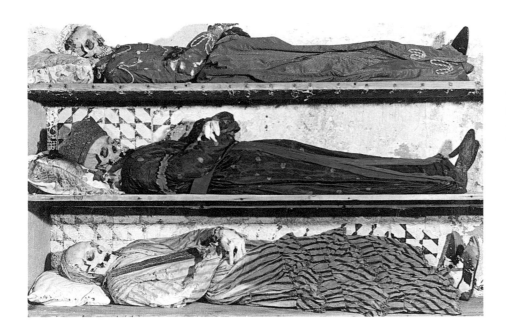

Hundreds of mummies—from little children to priests—are on display in Palermo, Sicily. Mummies are still tourist attractions in many parts of the world, but this is changing.

CHAPTER EIGHT

MUMMIES THEN AND NOW

A century ago, mummies were little more than oddities to most people. Thousands were shipped out of Egypt to decorate museums and private homes all over the world. One Englishman made a show-business career out of unwrapping mummies for his audiences!

Using human bodies as decorations, entertainment, or tourist attractions offends many people. The trend now is to preserve ancient bodies for scientific research.

In the United States, national parks and some museums no longer display human mummies at all. Many Native American groups do not like to have mummies of their ancestors put on display. For this reason, officials at Mammoth Cave National Park do not allow photos of mummies found there to be published.

Even so, mummies are still sometimes thought of as tourist attractions. Visitors to Palermo, Sicily, can tour a unique type of cemetery called a **catacomb.** This type of cemetery is built underground, like a basement with long halls. Spaces for the bodies are dug into the walls.

Palermo's Capuchin Catacombs are about 400 years old. These catacombs are cut from a form of rock that is very light and soaks up water, making the air in the tunnels very dry. Bodies placed in the catacombs dry naturally, but some of the 8,000 mummies have also been embalmed. Even though these people did not believe a body was necessary for life after death, they considered it an honor to be buried in the famous catacombs. Some families were comforted by seeing the body of a dead relative kept in a setting they thought was dignified.

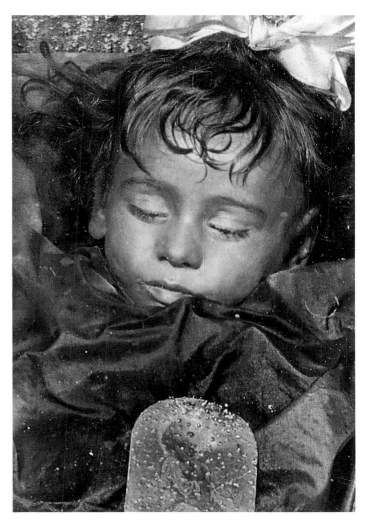

Looking as if she is just taking a nap, little Rosalia Lombardo actually died in 1920. After death, a doctor filled her body with chemicals. No one knows the exact process used, because the doctor is no longer living. Rosalia's body remains at the Capuchin Catacombs in Sicily.

Seeing the body of a dead relative or friend can help those left behind accept the death. In the United States, most bodies are now embalmed with chemicals soon after death. Preservation lasts only long enough for the body to be viewed at the funeral. Without embalming, funerals must be held within a day or so after death. Embalming allows relatives and friends from far away to see the body before it is buried if they wish.

Some people like the idea of being able to look at someone they loved any time they want, long after the person is dead. A few funeral directors are considering building special chapels where bodies would be preserved and stored. There, people would be able to see the mummified body of a family member for years to come. So far, it's only an idea.

Will mummification ever be as popular again as it was in ancient Egypt? We have the technology to preserve bodies for long periods of time, but it's too expensive for most people. All the same, it's likely some people from our time will become mummies.

Will the mummification of animals and people ever again be as popular as it was in ancient Egypt? That's one mystery these Egyptian animal mummies can't solve for us.

Besides modern embalming techniques like freeze-drying, natural conditions that preserved ancient mummies still exist today in the catacombs of Sicily and around the world.

Will future scientists study 20th-century mummies? The answer is probably yes. The mummy of a Japanese priest who died in this century has already been examined by scientists. Other well-preserved bodies are sure to provide clues about health, environment, and history.

Will it soon be possible to store a dead body and bring it back to life after a cure is found for whatever caused its death? The answer to that question is not as certain. While mummification can stop bodies from decaying, it cannot stop some of the changes that happen to tissues at death. Mummification does not preserve a body as it was in life, but only as it was at the time of death.

Mummies hold many clues about life in the past, but they also serve to remind us of death. By capturing the moment of death, mummies are a window into the greatest mystery of all—the mystery of life.

Few people in modern times want to be mummified, but some like the idea of keeping a favorite cat or dog around the house even if it's no longer alive. Chemical mummification of this cat, including the gold plating, cost its owner $5,000.

GLOSSARY

bitumen: a sticky substance found in the earth or made from petroleum. Bitumen is sometimes called asphalt, tar, or pitch. People in medieval Europe thought bitumen in Egyptian mummy wrappings could cure diseases.

bogs: areas formed when water is trapped in a pond and loses its oxygen. Waterlogged plants in a bog become trapped and decompose at the bottom, and peat mosses grow over the top. Bogs often preserve the people, animals, and things thrown into them.

canopic jars: special containers used by ancient Egyptians to hold the organs of a mummified body

catacomb: an underground cemetery. Bodies placed in catacombs in Palermo, Sicily, and Guanajuato, Mexico, have been mummified by natural conditions.

CT scans: sometimes called CAT scans, short for computerized axial tomography. This special kind of X ray uses computerized photography to show the inside of a body.

coffins: boxes or other containers in which dead bodies are buried. Most coffins in the United States are made of steel or wood, but in ancient Egypt stone coffins were common.

embalming: treating a dead body in order to preserve it from decay. Modern embalming generally only preserves the body until the funeral, but techniques such as freeze-drying can preserve bodies for longer periods.

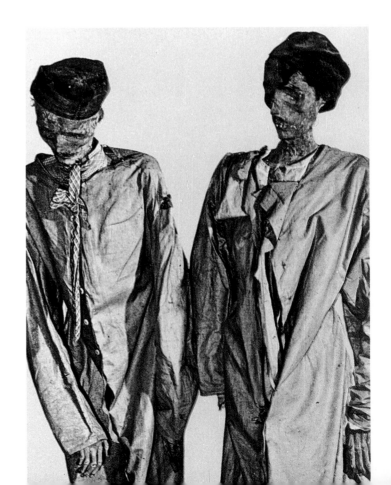

Natural conditions in the stone walls of the Capuchin Catacombs of Palermo, Sicily, preserved these mummies.

hieroglyphs: ancient Egyptian pictures that were part of an alphabet of picture writing

mummification: the process of turning a dead body into a mummy. Mummification occurs naturally—as when a body is quickly dried or frozen—or by embalming.

mummy: the body of a human or animal in which the soft tissues did not decay after death

mummy bundles: baskets, leather, or cloth coverings in which bodies from the Incan region of South America were wrapped for burial

mummy powder: medicine used during the Middle Ages, made by grinding up Egyptian mummy wrappings or whole mummies

natron: a saltlike mineral used in ancient times for embalming, for cleaning, and for making ceramic paste. When used in making Egyptian mummies, natron dried the body's tissues.

peat: a type of spongy soil formed when stagnant water and peat moss act on decomposing plants. Peat is found in bogs and can be used for fuel in stoves when cut into bricks and dried.

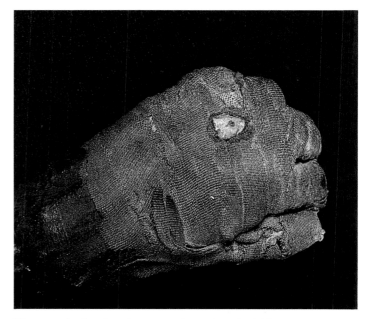

Rings and other jewelry were often placed within mummy wrappings in ancient Egypt.

pharaohs: ancient Egyptian rulers. During his lifetime, a pharaoh was thought to be the god-king of the living. At his death, his spirit was thought to become the god-king of the dead.

resin: a type of tree sap that is very sticky and becomes very hard when exposed to the air. Resin was used to form a hard outer coating on Egyptian mummies.

WHERE TO SEE MUMMIES

In 1977, Siberian miners found the frozen body of this baby mammoth. The mammoth, nicknamed "Dima," was about seven months old when it died, thousands of years ago. Dima is owned by the Zoological Museum of St. Petersburg in Russia.

Areas in North America where mummies have been found:

Canyon de Chelly National Monument, Chinle, AZ
Mammoth Cave National Park, Mammoth Cave, KY
Mesa Verde National Park, Mesa Verde, CO

Some museums in North America where mummies are on display:

Denver Museum of Natural History, Denver, CO
The Detroit Institute of Arts, Detroit, MI

Field Museum of Natural History, Chicago, IL
The Metropolitan Museum of Art, New York, NY
The Minneapolis Institute of Arts, Minneapolis, MN
Museum of Natural History, Smithsonian Institution, Washington, DC
Royal Ontario Museum, Toronto, Ontario, Canada
San Diego Museum of Man, San Diego, CA
The Science Museum of Minnesota, St. Paul, MN
St. Louis Art Museum, St. Louis, MO
University of Alaska Museum, Fairbanks, AK
The University Museum, Philadelphia, PA
Walters Art Gallery, Baltimore, MD

INDEX

ACKNOWLEDGMENTS

The author wishes to thank Arthur C. Aufderheide, M.D., Derek Notman, M.D., Robert Ward, the Science Museum of Minnesota, and the Minneapolis Institute of Arts.

CREDITS

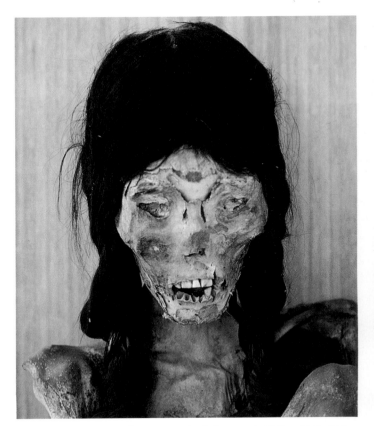

It's easy to see why this mummy's nickname is "Miss Chile." She must have been beautiful during her life.